Classic
Italian

COMPREHENSIVE, STEP-BY-STEP COOKING

hinkler

Published by Hinkler Books Pty Ltd
45–55 Fairchild Street
Heatherton Victoria 3202 Australia
www.hinkler.com.au

hinkler

© A.C.N. 144 619 894 Pty Ltd 2012

Design: Hinkler Design Studio
Typesetting: MPS Limited
Prepress: Graphic Print Group

ISBN: 978 1 7430 8870 8

Printed and bound in China

Contents

SPAGHETTI BOLOGNESE

Preparation time:
10 minutes

Cooking time:
55 minutes

Serves 4

INGREDIENTS

- 1 tablespoon olive oil
- 1 large onion, diced
- 2 garlic cloves, crushed
- 600 g (1 lb 5 oz) minced (ground) beef
- ½ cup (125 ml/4¼ fl oz) red wine
- ½ cup (125 ml/4¼ fl oz) beef stock (broth)
- 2 × 400 g (14 oz) cans chopped tomatoes
- 1 carrot, grated
- 350 g (12¼ oz) spaghetti

1 Heat the oil over medium heat in a large saucepan, add the onion and garlic and cook for 1–2 minutes, or until soft. Add the meat and cook, stirring to break up any lumps, for 5 minutes, or until the meat is browned. Pour in the wine and simmer for 2–3 minutes, or until reduced slightly, then add the stock (broth) and simmer for 2 minutes. Add the tomato and carrot and season well. Cook over low heat for 40 minutes.

2 About 15 minutes before serving, cook the pasta in a large saucepan of boiling water until *al dente*. Drain well and keep warm. Divide the pasta evenly among four serving bowls and pour the meat sauce over the pasta. Garnish with parsley, if desired.

HINT: Delicious with grated Parmesan cheese.

LINGUINE WITH HAM, ARTICHOKE AND LEMON SAUCE

Preparation time:
15 minutes

Cooking time:
10 minutes

Serves 4

INGREDIENTS

- 500 g (1 lb 2 oz) fresh linguine
- 25 g (¾ oz) butter
- 2 large garlic cloves, chopped
- 150 g (5¼ oz) marinated artichokes, drained and quartered
- 150 g (5¼ oz) sliced leg ham, cut into strips
- 300 ml (10 fl oz) cream
- 2 teaspoons coarsely grated lemon zest
- ½ cup (15 g/½ oz) fresh basil, torn
- ⅓ cup (35 g/1¼ oz) grated Parmesan cheese

1 Cook the pasta in a large saucepan of boiling water until *al dente*. Drain, then return to the pan. Meanwhile, melt the butter in a large frying pan, add the garlic and cook over medium heat for 1 minute, or until fragrant. Add the artichokes and ham and cook for a further 2 minutes.

2 Add the cream and lemon zest, reduce the heat and simmer for 5 minutes, gently breaking up the artichokes with a spoon. Pour the sauce over the pasta, then add the basil and Parmesan and toss until the pasta is evenly coated. Divide among four serving plates and serve.

ANGEL HAIR PASTA WITH SCALLOPS

Preparation time:
15 minutes

Cooking time:
15 minutes

Serves 4

INGREDIENTS

- 350 g (12¼ oz) angel hair pasta
- 100 g (3½ oz) butter
- 3 garlic cloves, crushed
- 24 scallops, without roe
- 150 g (5¼ oz) baby rocket (arugula) leaves
- 2 teaspoons finely grated lemon zest
- ¼ cup (60 ml/2 fl oz) lemon juice
- 125 g (4⅓ oz) semi-dried (sun-blushed) tomatoes, thinly sliced
- 30 g (1 oz) shaved Parmesan cheese

1 Cook the pasta in a large saucepan of boiling water until *al dente*. Meanwhile, melt the butter in a small saucepan, add the garlic and cook over low heat, stirring, for 1 minute. Remove from the heat.

2 Heat a lightly greased chargrill (charbroil) plate over high heat and cook the scallops, brushing occasionally with some of the garlic butter for 1–2 minutes each side, or until cooked. Set aside and keep warm.

3 Drain the pasta and return to the pan with the remaining garlic butter, the rocket (arugula), lemon zest, lemon juice and tomato and toss until combined. Divide among four serving plates and top with the scallops. Season to taste and sprinkle with Parmesan.

SPAGHETTI NICOISE

Preparation time:
10 minutes

Cooking time:
15 minutes

Serves 4–6

INGREDIENTS

- 350 g (12¼ oz) spaghetti
- 8 quail eggs (or 4 hen eggs)
- 1 lemon
- 3 × 185 g (6½ oz) cans good-quality tuna in oil
- ⅓ cup (50 g / 1¾ oz) pitted and halved Kalamata olives
- 100 g (3½ oz) semi-dried (sun-blushed) tomatoes, cut lengthways
- 4 anchovy fillets, chopped into small pieces
- 3 tablespoons baby capers, drained
- 3 tablespoons chopped fresh flat-leaf (Italian) parsley

1 Cook the pasta in a large saucepan of boiling water until *al dente*. Meanwhile, place the eggs in a saucepan of cold water, bring to the boil and cook for 4 minutes (10 minutes for hen eggs). Drain, cool under cold water, then peel. Cut the quail eggs into halves or the hen eggs into quarters. Finely grate the rind of the lemon to give 1 teaspoon of grated zest. Then, squeeze the lemon to give 2 tablespoons juice.

2 Empty the tuna and its oil into a large bowl. Add the olives, tomato halves, anchovies, lemon zest and juice, capers and 2 tablespoons of the parsley. Drain the pasta and rinse in a little cold water, then toss gently through the tuna mixture. Divide among serving bowls, garnish with egg and the extra chopped fresh parsley, and serve.

CREAMY TOMATO AND BACON PASTA

Preparation time:
10 minutes

Cooking time:
15 minutes

Serves 4

INGREDIENTS

- 400 g (14 oz) cresti di gallo
- 1 tablespoon olive oil
- 170 g (6 oz) streaky bacon, thinly sliced (see NOTE)
- 500 g (1 lb 2 oz) Roma (plum or egg-shaped) tomatoes, roughly chopped
- ½ cup (125 ml/4¼ fl oz) thick (double/heavy) cream
- 2 tablespoons sun-dried (sun-blushed) tomato pesto
- 2 tablespoons finely chopped fresh flat-leaf (Italian) parsley
- ½ cup (50 g/1¾ oz) finely grated Parmesan cheese

1 Cook the pasta in a large saucepan of boiling water until *al dente*. Drain and return to the pan. Meanwhile, heat the oil in a frying pan, add the bacon and cook over high heat for 2 minutes, or until starting to brown. Reduce the heat to medium, add the tomato and cook, stirring frequently, for 2 minutes, or until the tomato has softened but still holds its shape.

2 Stir in the cream and pesto until heated through. Remove from heat, add the parsley, then toss the sauce and Parmesan through the pasta.

NOTE: Streaky bacon is the tail end of bacon rashers. It is fattier but adds to the flavour of the meal. You can use 170 g (6 oz) bacon rashers if you prefer.

SPAGHETTI MARINARA

Preparation time:
15 minutes

Cooking time:
35 minutes

Serves 4–6

INGREDIENTS

- 2 tablespoons olive oil
- 1 onion, finely chopped
- 2 garlic cloves, crushed
- 2 × 400 g (14 oz) cans chopped tomatoes
- ¼ cup (60 g / 2 oz) tomato paste (tomato puree)
- 500 g (1 lb 2 oz) spaghetti
- 500 g (1 lb 2 oz) good-quality marinara mix (see NOTE)
- 8 black mussels, beards removed, scrubbed
- 2 tablespoons shredded fresh basil

1 Heat the oil in a saucepan over medium heat, add the onion and cook for 5 minutes, or until softened and lightly browned. Add the garlic and stir for another 1 minute, or until aromatic. Add the tomato and tomato paste (tomato puree) and bring to the boil, then reduce the heat and simmer for 20–25 minutes, or until the sauce becomes rich and pulpy. Stir the sauce occasionally during cooking. Season with salt and ground black pepper. Meanwhile, cook the pasta in a large saucepan of boiling water until *al dente*. Drain well, return to the saucepan and keep warm.

2 Add the marinara mix and the mussels to the tomato sauce and cook for about 2–3 minutes, or until the seafood is cooked and the mussels are open. Discard any mussels that do not open. Stir in the basil. Toss the sauce through the warm pasta and serve.

NOTE: Marinara mix is available from seafood stores. Try to choose a good-quality marinara mix to avoid chewy seafood. Alternatively, you can make your own by choosing a few different types of seafood, such as octopus, fish fillets and calamari, and chopping into bite-size pieces.

ROASTED BUTTERNUT SAUCE ON PAPPARDELLE

Preparation time:
15 minutes

Cooking time:
35 minutes

Serves 4

INGREDIENTS

- 1.4 kg (3 lb 1 oz) butternut pumpkin (squash), cut into 2 cm (¾ inch) pieces
- 4 garlic cloves, crushed
- 3 teaspoons fresh thyme leaves
- 100 ml (3½ fl oz) olive oil
- 500 g (1 lb 2 oz) pappardelle
- 2 tablespoons cream
- ¾ cup (185 ml/6½ fl oz) hot chicken stock (broth)
- 30 g (1 oz) shaved Parmesan cheese

1 Preheat the oven to 200°C (400°F/Gas 6). Place the pumpkin (squash), garlic, thyme and ¼ cup (60 ml/2 fl oz) of the olive oil in a bowl and toss together. Season with salt, transfer to a baking tray (sheet) and cook for 30 minutes, or until tender and golden. Meanwhile, cook the pasta in a large saucepan of boiling water until *al dente*. Drain and return to the pan. Toss through the remaining oil and keep warm.

2 Place the cooked pumpkin (squash) and the cream in a food processor or blender and process until smooth. Add the hot stock (broth) and process until smooth and combined. Season with salt and ground black pepper and gently toss through the warm pasta. Divide among four serving plates, sprinkle with Parmesan and extra thyme leaves, if desired, and serve immediately.

NOTE: The sauce becomes gluggy on standing, so serve it as soon as possible.

GARLIC AND CHILLI OIL SPAGHETTI

Preparation time:
15 minutes

Cooking time:
15 minutes

Serves 4–6

INGREDIENTS

- 1 cup (250 ml/8½ fl oz) good-quality olive oil
- 2 bird's eye chillies, seeded and thinly sliced
- 5–6 large cloves garlic, crushed
- 500 g (1 lb 2 oz) spaghetti
- 100 g (3½ oz) thinly sliced prosciutto
- ½ cup (30 g/1 oz) chopped fresh flat-leaf (Italian) parsley
- 2 tablespoons chopped fresh basil
- 2 tablespoons chopped fresh oregano
- ¾ cup (75 g/2⅔ oz) good-quality grated Parmesan cheese

1 Pour the oil into a small saucepan with the chilli and garlic. Slowly heat the oil over low heat for about 12 minutes to infuse the oil with the garlic and chilli. Don't allow the oil to reach smoking point or the garlic will burn and taste bitter.

2 Meanwhile, cook the pasta in a large saucepan of boiling water until *al dente*. Drain well and return to the pan. Lay the prosciutto on a grill (broiler) tray and cook under a hot grill (broiler) for 2 minutes each side, or until crispy. Cool and break into pieces.

3 Pour the hot oil mixture over the spaghetti and toss well with the prosciutto, fresh herbs and Parmesan. Season to taste.

NOTE: This is a very simple dish, but it relies on good-quality ingredients.

PASTA GNOCCHI WITH SAUSAGE

Preparation time:
15 minutes

Cooking time:
20 minutes

Serves 4–6

INGREDIENTS

- 500 g (1 lb 2 oz) pasta gnocchi
- 2 tablespoons olive oil
- 400 g (14 oz) thin Italian sausages
- 1 red onion, finely chopped
- 2 garlic cloves, finely chopped
- 2 × 400 g (14 oz) cans chopped tomatoes
- 1 teaspoon caster (berry) sugar
- 35 g (1¼ oz) fresh basil, torn
- ½ cup (45 g / 1⅔ oz) grated pecorino cheese

1 Cook the pasta in a large saucepan of boiling water until *al dente*. Drain and return the pasta to the pan. Meanwhile, heat 2 teaspoons of the oil in a large frying pan. Add the sausages and cook, turning, for 5 minutes, or until well browned and cooked through. Drain on paper towels, then slice when they have cooled enough to touch. Keep warm.

2 Wipe clean the frying pan and heat the remaining oil. Add the onion and garlic and cook over medium heat for 2 minutes, or until the onion has softened. Add the tomato, sugar and 1 cup (250 ml / 8½ fl oz) water and season well with ground black pepper. Reduce the heat and simmer for 12 minutes, or until thickened and reduced a little.

3 Pour the sauce over the cooked pasta and stir through the sausage, then the basil and half of the cheese. Divide among serving plates and serve hot with the remaining cheese sprinkled over the top.

SPINACH RAVIOLI WITH PINE NUT SALSA

Preparation time:
15 minutes

Cooking time:
10 minutes

Serves 4

INGREDIENTS

- 625 g (1 lb 6 oz) spinach ravioli
- 3½ tablespoons olive oil
- ⅓ cup (50 g/1¾ oz) pine nuts
- 150 g (5¼ oz) semi-dried (sun-blushed) tomatoes, thinly sliced
- 270 g (9½ oz) jar roasted capsicums (peppers), drained and thinly sliced
- 2 tablespoons finely chopped fresh flat-leaf (Italian) parsley
- 2 tablespoons finely chopped fresh mint
- 1½ tablespoons balsamic vinegar
- 30 g (1 oz) shaved Parmesan cheese

1 Cook the pasta in a large saucepan of boiling water until *al dente*. Drain. Heat ½ teaspoon of the oil in a frying pan and gently cook the pine nuts until light gold. Remove from the pan and roughly chop.

2 Add the remaining oil to the pan and add the tomato, capsicum (pepper), parsley, mint and vinegar and stir until combined and warmed through. Remove from the heat and season to taste. Stir in the pine nuts. Divide the pasta among four serving plates, spoon on the sauce and top with the Parmesan. Serve immediately.

RAVIOLI IN ROASTED VEGETABLE SAUCE

Preparation time:
15 minutes

Cooking time:
15 minutes

Serves 4

INGREDIENTS

- 6 red capsicums (peppers)
- 6 slices prosciutto
- 625 g (1 lb 6 oz) chicken or ricotta ravioli
- 2 tablespoons olive oil
- 3 garlic cloves, crushed
- 2 leeks, thinly sliced
- 1 tablespoon chopped fresh oregano
- 2 teaspoons soft brown sugar
- 1 cup (250 ml/8½ fl oz) hot chicken stock (broth)

1 Cut the capsicums (peppers) into large pieces, removing the seeds and membrane. Place, skin-side-up, under a hot grill (broiler) until the skin blackens and blisters. Cool in a plastic bag, then peel away the skin.

Place the prosciutto under the grill (broiler) and cook for 1 minute each side, or until crisp. Break into pieces and set aside.

2 Cook the pasta in a large saucepan of boiling water until *al dente*. Meanwhile, heat the oil in a frying pan and cook the garlic and leek over medium heat for 3–4 minutes, or until softened. Add the oregano and sugar and stir for 1 minute.

3 Place the capsicum (pepper) and leek mixture in a food processor or blender, season with salt and pepper and process until combined. Add the chicken stock (broth) and process until smooth. Drain the pasta and return to the saucepan. Gently toss the sauce through the ravioli over low heat until warmed through. Divide among four serving bowls and sprinkle with prosciutto.

TORTELLINI WITH MUSHROOM SAUCE

Preparation time:
15 minutes

Cooking time:
20 minutes

Serves 4

INGREDIENTS

- 500 g (1 lb 2 oz) tortellini
- ¼ cup (60 ml/2 fl oz) olive oil
- 600 g (1 lb 5 oz) Swiss brown mushrooms, thinly sliced
- 2 garlic cloves, crushed
- ½ cup (125 ml/4¼ fl oz) dry white wine
- 300 ml (10 fl oz) thick (double/heavy) cream
- pinch ground nutmeg
- 3 tablespoons finely chopped fresh flat-leaf (Italian) parsley
- 30 g (1 oz) grated Parmesan cheese

1 Cook the pasta in a large saucepan of boiling water until *al dente*. Drain. Meanwhile, heat the oil in a frying pan over medium heat. Add the mushrooms and cook, stirring occasionally, for 5 minutes, or until softened. Add the garlic and cook for 1 minute, then stir in the wine and cook for 5 minutes, or until the liquid has reduced by half.

2 Add the cream, nutmeg and parsley, stir to combine and cook for 3–5 minutes, or until it thickens slightly. Season. Divide the tortellini among four bowls and spoon on the sauce and sprinkle with Parmesan.

AGNOLOTTI WITH ALFREDO SAUCE

Preparation time:
10 minutes

Cooking time:
10 minutes

Serves 4–6

INGREDIENTS

- 625 g (1 lb 6 oz) agnolotti
- 90 g (3¼ oz) butter
- 1½ cups (150 g/5¼ oz) grated Parmesan cheese
- 300 ml (10 fl oz) cream
- 2 tablespoons chopped fresh marjoram

1 Cook the pasta in a large saucepan of boiling water until *al dente*. Drain and return to the pan.

2 Just before the pasta is cooked, melt the butter in a saucepan over low heat. Add the Parmesan and cream and bring to the boil. Reduce the heat and simmer, stirring constantly, for 2 minutes, or until the sauce has thickened slightly. Stir in the marjoram and season with salt and ground black pepper. Toss the sauce through the pasta until well coated and serve immediately.

VARIATION: Marjoram can be replaced with any other fresh herb you prefer – for example, try parsley, thyme, chervil or dill (dill weed).

CREAMY PASTA BAKE

Preparation time:
15 minutes

Cooking time:
40 minutes

Serves 4

INGREDIENTS

- 200 g (7 oz) risoni
- 40 g (1½ oz) butter
- 4 spring (green) onions, thinly sliced
- 400 g (14 oz) zucchini (courgettes), grated
- 4 eggs
- ½ cup (125 ml/4¼ fl oz) cream
- 100 g (3½ oz) ricotta cheese (see NOTE)
- ⅔ cup (100 g/3½ oz) grated mozzarella cheese
- ¾ cup (75 g/2⅔ oz) grated Parmesan cheese

1 Preheat the oven to 180°C (350°F/Gas 4). Cook the pasta in a large saucepan of boiling water until *al dente*. Drain well. Meanwhile, heat the butter in a frying pan, cook the spring (green) onion for 1 minute, then add the zucchini (courgette) and cook for a further 4 minutes, or until soft. Cool slightly.

2 Combine the eggs, cream, ricotta, mozzarella, risoni and half of the Parmesan well. Stir in the zucchini (courgette) mixture. Season. Spoon into four 2 cup (500 ml/17 fl oz) greased ovenproof dishes, but not to the brim. Sprinkle with the remaining Parmesan and cook for 25–30 minutes, or until firm and golden.

NOTE: With such simple flavours, it is important to use good-quality fresh ricotta from the delicatessen or the deli section of your local supermarket.

MUSHROOM AND RICOTTA CANNELLONI

Preparation time:
15 minutes

Cooking time:
30 minutes

Serves 4

INGREDIENTS

- 500 g (1 lb 2 oz) button mushrooms
- 200 g (7 oz) fresh lasagne sheets
- 2 tablespoons olive oil
- 3 garlic cloves, crushed
- 2 tablespoons lemon juice
- 400 g (14 oz) fresh ricotta cheese
- 3 tablespoons chopped fresh basil
- 425 g (15 oz) bottled tomato pasta (marinara) sauce
- 1 cup (150 g/5¼ oz) grated mozzarella cheese

1 Preheat the oven to 180°C (350°F/Gas 4). Place the mushrooms in a food processor and pulse until finely chopped. Cut the lasagne sheets into twelve 13 × 16 cm (5 × 6⅓ inch) rectangles.

2 Heat the oil in a large frying pan over medium heat. Add the garlic and mushrooms and cook, stirring, for 3 minutes. Add the lemon juice and cook for 2 minutes, or until softened. Transfer to a sieve over a bowl to collect the juices, pressing with a spoon to remove as much moisture as possible. Reserve.

3 Combine the mushrooms, ricotta and basil. Season well. Place heaped tablespoons of the mixture along one long edge of the lasagne sheet. Roll up, then place in a greased 8 cup (2 litre/2.1 US qt/1.75 UK qt) 16 × 30 cm (6⅓ × 12 inch) ovenproof ceramic dish. Repeat with the remaining mixture and sheets, placing them in a single layer. Pour on the reserved mushroom cooking liquid, then pour on the pasta sauce. Sprinkle with cheese and bake for 25 minutes, or until golden and bubbling. Serve with salad.

PROSCIUTTO AND SPINACH LASAGNE

Preparation time:
15 minutes + 10 minutes standing

Cooking time:
25 minutes

Serves 4–6

INGREDIENTS

- 600 g (1 lb 5 oz) bottled tomato pasta (marinara) sauce
- 250 g (8¾ oz) fresh lasagne sheets
- 400 g (14 oz) bocconcini, thinly sliced
- 500 g (1 lb 2 oz) English (common) spinach, trimmed
- ½ cup (125 ml/4¼ fl oz) cream
- 10 thin slices prosciutto, chopped
- 1 cup (150 g/5¼ oz) grated mozzarella cheese
- ½ cup (50 g/1¾ oz) finely grated Parmesan cheese

1 Preheat the oven to 180°C (350°F/Gas 4). Lightly grease a 12 cup (3 litre/3.2 US qt/2.6 UK qt) shallow 23 cm × 30 cm (9 × 12 inch) ovenproof dish. Spread half of the tomato pasta (marinara) sauce over the base of the dish. Cover the layer of pasta sauce with a third of the lasagne sheets. Top with half of the bocconcini and half of the spinach. Drizzle on half of the cream and sprinkle with half of the prosciutto. Season with some salt and ground black pepper. Repeat to give two layers, starting with half of the remaining lasagne sheets.

2 Lay the final layer of lasagne over the top and spread with the remaining pasta sauce. Sprinkle with the combined mozzarella and Parmesan. Bake for 25 minutes, or until cooked. Leave to stand for 10 minutes before serving.

ROASTED TOMATO AND OREGANO PIZZA

Preparation time:
40 minutes

Total cooking time:
1 hour 45 minutes

Serves 4

INGREDIENTS

- 500 g (1 lb 2 oz) plum (egg-shaped) tomatoes
- 1 large eggplant (aubergine)
- olive oil, for frying
- 200 g (7 oz) mozzarella, grated
- ¼ cup (25 g/¾ oz) grated Parmesan
- 1 tablespoon chopped fresh oregano

PIZZA BASE
- 1 teaspoon dried yeast
- ¼ teaspoon salt
- ¼ teaspoon sugar
- 1¼ cups (155 g/5½ oz) plain (all-purpose) flour
- 6 cloves garlic, crushed

1 Preheat the oven to slow 150°C (300°F/Gas 2). Cut the tomatoes in half and place in one layer on a baking tray (sheet), cut-side-up. Sprinkle with salt and roast for 1 hour 15 minutes. Set aside to cool.

2 To make Pizza Base: Put the yeast, salt, sugar and ½ cup (125 ml/4¼ fl oz) warm water in a small bowl. Leave, covered with plastic wrap, in a warm place for 10 minutes, or until foamy. Sift the flour into a large bowl, make a well in the centre and add the yeast mixture and garlic. Mix to form a dough. Knead on a lightly floured surface for 10 minutes, or until smooth and elastic. Roll out to fit a 30 cm (12 inch) greased or non-stick pizza tray (sheet).

3 Preheat the oven to moderately hot 200°C (400°F/Gas 6). Thinly slice the eggplant (aubergine). Drizzle a char-grill (char-broiler) or large frying pan with olive oil until nearly smoking. Add the eggplant (aubergine) in batches and cook, turning once, until soft (brush with a little more oil if it starts to stick). Drain on paper towels.

4 Arrange the eggplant
  (aubergine) on the pizza base.
  Top with tomatoes and sprinkle
  with the combined mozzarella and
  Parmesan. Bake for

20–30 minutes, or until the base
is cooked and the cheese melted
and golden. Sprinkle with fresh
oregano to serve.

OLIVE AND ONION TART

Preparation time:
25 minutes

Total cooking time:
35–40 minutes

Serves 4–6

INGREDIENTS

- 1 teaspoon sugar
- 1½ teaspoons dried yeast
- ½ cup (125 ml/4¼ fl oz) olive oil
- 5 onions, thinly sliced
- 1 cup (125 g/4⅓ oz) self-raising flour
- ½ cup (125 g/4⅓ oz) plain (all-purpose) white flour
- 1 cup (185 g/6½ oz) black (ripe) olives
- 2 tablespoons grated Parmesan cheese

1 Dissolve the sugar in ½ cup (125 ml/4¼ fl oz) warm water. Sprinkle with yeast and leave for 10 minutes, or until frothy.

2 Heat 3 tablespoons oil in a frying pan and fry the onion for 10 minutes, or until soft. Leave to cool. Preheat the oven to hot 220°C (425°F/Gas 7).

3 Sift together the self-raising flour, plain (all-purpose) flour and a good pinch of salt in a bowl. Make a well in the centre and pour in the yeast mixture and 2 tablespoons oil. Bring together to form a dough and knead on a lightly floured surface for 10 minutes, or until smooth. Extra flour may be necessary.

4 Roll out the dough to line a greased 30 cm (12 inch) pizza tray (sheet). Spread with cooked onions, then olives. Brush the crust with the remaining olive oil. Bake for 25–30 minutes. Serve hot or cold, sprinked with grated Parmesan.

SUN-DRIED TOMATO AND SALAMI PIZZA

Preparation time:
40 minutes

Total cooking time:
35–45 minutes

Serves 4

INGREDIENTS

- 1 green capsicum (pepper)
- 1 red or yellow capsicum (pepper)
- 1 cup (125 g/4⅓ oz) grated Cheddar (American) cheese
- 100 g (3½ oz) salami, sliced
- 1 red onion, thinly sliced into rings
- ½ cup (90 g/3¼ oz) black (ripe) olives, pitted and sliced
- 150 g (5¼ oz) bocconcini

PIZZA BASE
- 7 g (¼ oz) sachet dried yeast
- ½ teaspoon salt
- ½ teaspoon sugar
- 2½ cups (250 g/8¾ oz) plain (all-purpose) flour
- 1 cup (160 g/5⅔ oz) sun-dried tomatoes, finely chopped
- ½ cup (80 g/2¾ oz) pine nuts, finely chopped

1 Cut the capsicums (peppers) into large flat pieces; remove the membrane and seeds. Place, skin-side-up, under a hot grill (broiler) and cook until the skin blackens and blisters. Cool under a tea towel. Peel away the skin and cut the flesh into thin strips. Set aside.

2 **To make Pizza Base:** Mix the yeast, salt, sugar and 1 cup (250 ml/8½ fl oz) warm water in a small bowl. Cover with plastic wrap and leave in a warm place for 10 minutes, until foamy. Sift the flour into a bowl, make a well in the centre and add the yeast mixture, sun-dried tomatoes and pine nuts. Mix to a dough.

3 Preheat the oven to moderately hot 200°C (400°F/Gas 6). Knead the dough on a lightly floured surface for about 10 minutes, or until smooth and elastic. Roll out to a 35 cm (14 inch) round. Place on a 30 cm (12 inch) non-stick pizza tray (sheet), folding the edge over to form a rim.

4 Sprinkle the pizza base with grated cheese. Top with salami, red onion, olives and roasted capsicum (pepper). Bake for 30–40 minutes, or until the base is cooked. Top with thinly sliced bocconcini and bake for a further 5 minutes, or until just melted.

VARIATION: Use sun-dried capsicum (pepper) instead of tomato in the pizza base.

POTATO ONION PIZZA

Preparation time:
40 minutes

Total cooking time:
40 minutes

Serves 4

INGREDIENTS

- 7 g (¼ oz) sachet dry yeast
- ½ teaspoon sugar
- 1½ cups (185 g/6½ oz) plain (all-purpose) flour
- 1 cup (150 g/5¼ oz) wholemeal plain (whole wheat all-purpose) flour
- 1 tablespoon olive oil

TOPPING
- 1 large red capsicum (pepper)
- 1 potato, peeled
- 1 large onion, sliced
- 125 g (4⅓ oz) soft goat's cheese, crumbled
- 3 tablespoons capers
- 1 tablespoon dried oregano
- 1 teaspoon cracked pepper
- 1 teaspoon olive oil

1 Mix the yeast, sugar, a good pinch of salt and 1 cup (250 ml/8½ fl oz) warm water in a bowl. Cover with plastic wrap and leave in a warm place for 10 minutes, or until foamy. Sift both flours into a bowl. Make a well in the centre, add the yeast mixture and mix to a firm dough. Knead on a lightly floured surface for 5 minutes, or until smooth. Roll out to a 35 cm (14 inch) round. Brush a 30 cm (12 inch) pizza tray (sheet) with oil; put the dough on the tray (sheet) and tuck the edge over to form a rim. Preheat the oven to moderately hot 200°C (400°F/Gas 6).

2 **To make Topping:** Cut the capsicum (pepper) into large flat pieces; remove the seeds. Place, skin-side-up, under a hot grill (broiler) until blackened. Cool under a tea towel, peel away the skin and cut the flesh into narrow strips.

3 Slice the potato paper thin and arrange over the base with the onion, capsicum (pepper) and half the goat's cheese. Sprinkle with capers, oregano and pepper and drizzle with olive oil. Brush the edge of the crust with oil and bake for 20 minutes. Add the remaining goat's cheese and bake for 15–20 minutes, or until the crust has browned. Cut into wedges to serve.

NOTE: Goat's cheese, also known as Chèvre, is available at delicatessens.

HAM AND CHEESE CALZONE

Preparation time:
30 minutes + chilling
Total cooking time:
30 minutes
Makes 4

INGREDIENTS

- 2 cups (250 g/8¾ oz) plain (all-purpose) flour
- 100 g (3½ oz) butter, chopped
- 2 egg yolks

HAM AND CHEESE FILLING
- 250 g (8¾ oz) ricotta cheese
- 50 g (1¼ oz) Gruyère cheese, cubed
- 50 g (1¼ oz) ham, finely chopped
- 2 spring (green) onions, chopped
- 1 tablespoon chopped fresh flat-leaf parsley
- freshly ground black pepper

1 Lightly grease a large oven tray (sheet). Sift the flour and a pinch of salt into a bowl and rub in the butter. Make a well in the centre, cut in the egg yolks with a knife and add 2–3 tablespoons water, or enough to form a dough. Gather together into a ball, cover with plastic wrap and chill for 20 minutes. Preheat the oven to moderately hot 200°C (400°F/ Gas 6).

2 **To make Filling:** Combine the cheeses, ham, spring (green) onions, parsley and black pepper in a bowl.

3 Roll out a quarter of the dough to make a large round 3 mm (⅛ inch) thick, trimming any uneven edges. Spoon a quarter of the filling mixture into the centre, brush the edge very lightly with water and fold over to enclose the filling, pressing the edge to seal. Repeat with the remaining dough and filling. Place the Calzone on the oven tray (sheet), brush with a little olive oil and bake for 30 minutes, or until well browned and crisp.

NOTE: Calzone can be made 1 day ahead and kept refrigerated before baking. Pastry can be made in a food processor, in short bursts.

CARROT AND PUMPKIN RISOTTO

Preparation time:
15 minutes

Total cooking time:
35 minutes

Serves 4

INGREDIENTS

- 90 g (3¼ oz) butter
- 1 onion, finely chopped
- 250 g (8¾ oz) pumpkin, peeled and cut into small cubes
- 2 carrots, cut into small cubes
- 7–8 cups (1.75–2 litres; 1.8 US qt/ 1.5 UK qt–2.1 US qt/1.8 UK qt) vegetable stock (broth)
- 2 cups (440 g/15½ oz) arborio rice
- 90 g (3¼ oz) freshly grated Romano cheese
- ¼ teaspoon nutmeg
- freshly ground black pepper

1 Heat 60 g (2 oz) of the butter in a large, heavy-based pan. Add the onion and fry for 1–2 minutes, or until soft. Add the pumpkin and carrot and cook for 6–8 minutes, or until tender. Mash slightly with a potato masher. In a separate saucepan keep the stock (broth) at simmering point.

2 Add the rice to the vegetables and cook for 1 minute, stirring constantly. Ladle in enough hot stock (broth) to cover the rice; stir well. Reduce the heat and add more stock (broth) as it is absorbed, stirring frequently. Continue until the rice is tender and creamy (about 25 minutes).

3 Remove from the heat, add the remaining butter, cheese, nutmeg and pepper and fork through. Cover and leave for 5 minutes before serving.

NOTE: Romano is a hard, grating cheese similar to Parmesan.

PRAWN SAFFRON RISOTTO

Preparation time:
20 minutes

Total cooking time:
40 minutes

Serves 4

INGREDIENTS

- ¼ teaspoon saffron threads
- 500 g (1 lb 2 oz) raw prawns (shrimp)
- ⅓ cup (80 ml/2¾ fl oz) olive oil
- 2 cloves garlic, crushed
- 3 tablespoons chopped parsley
- 3 tablespoons dry sherry
- 3 tablespoons white wine
- 6 cups (1.5 litres/1.6 US qt/ 1.3 UK qt) fish stock (broth)
- 1 onion, diced
- 2 cups (440 g/15½ oz) arborio rice

1 Soak the saffron threads in 3 tablespoons water. Peel the prawns (shrimp) and devein, leaving the tails intact. Heat 2 tablespoons of the olive oil in a pan. Add the garlic, parsley and prawns (shrimp) and season with salt and pepper, to taste. Cook for 2 minutes, then add the sherry, wine and saffron threads with their liquid. Remove the prawns (shrimp) with a slotted spoon. Simmer until the liquid has reduced by half. Add the fish stock (broth) and 1 cup (250 ml/8½ fl oz) water and leave to simmer.

2 In a separate large, heavy-based pan heat the remaining oil. Add the onion and rice and cook for 3 minutes. Keeping the pan of stock (broth) constantly at simmering point, add ½ cup (125 ml/4¼ oz) hot stock (broth) to the rice mixture. Stir constantly over low heat, with a wooden spoon, until all the liquid has been absorbed. Add another half cupful of stock (broth) and repeat the process until all the stock (broth) has been added and the rice is tender and creamy – this will take 25–30 minutes.

3 Stir in the prawns (shrimp), warm through and serve, perhaps with freshly grated Parmesan cheese.

NOTE: Saffron is the most expensive spice in the world but only a very tiny amount is necessary.

MUSHROOM AND PANCETTA RISOTTO

Preparation time:
15 minutes

Cooking time:
35 minutes

Serves 4–6

INGREDIENTS

- 25 g (¾ oz) butter
- 2 garlic cloves, finely chopped
- 150 g (5¼ oz) piece pancetta, diced
- 400 g (14 oz) button mushrooms, sliced
- 500 g (1 lb 2 oz) risoni
- 1 litre (1.1 US qt/1.75 UK qt) chicken stock (broth)
- 125 ml (4¼ fl oz) cream
- 50 g (1¾ oz) finely grated Parmesan cheese
- 4 tablespoons finely chopped fresh flat-leaf (Italian) parsley

1 Melt the butter in a saucepan, add the garlic and cook over medium heat for 30 seconds, then increase the heat to high, add the pancetta and cook for 3–5 minutes, or until crisp. Add the mushrooms and cook for 3–5 minutes, or until softened.

2 Add the risoni, stir until coated in the mixture. Add the stock (broth) and bring to the boil. Reduce the heat to medium and cook, covered, for 15–20 minutes, or until nearly all the liquid has evaporated and the risoni is tender.

3 Stir in the cream and cook, uncovered, for a further 3 minutes, stirring occasionally until the cream is absorbed. Stir in ⅓ cup (35g/1¼ oz) of the Parmesan and all the parsley and season to taste. Divide among four serving bowls and serve sprinkled with the remaining Parmesan.

PANNA COTTA WITH RUBY SAUCE

Preparation time:
20 minutes + chilling

Total cooking time:
20 minutes

Serves 6

INGREDIENTS

- 1½ cups (375 ml/13 fl oz) milk
- 3 teaspoons gelatine
- 1½ cups (375 ml/13 fl oz) cream
- ⅓ cup (90 g/3¼ oz) caster (berry) sugar
- 2 tablespoons amaretto (almond-flavoured) liqueur

RUBY SAUCE
- 1 cup (250 g/8¾ oz) caster (berry) sugar
- 1 cinnamon stick
- 1 cup fresh or frozen raspberries
- ½ cup (125 ml/4¼ fl oz) good-quality red wine

1 Use your fingertips to lightly smear the inside of 6 individual 150 ml (5 fl oz) moulds with almond or light olive oil. Place 3 tablespoons of the milk in a small bowl and sprinkle with gelatine; leave to dissolve for a few minutes.

2 Put the remaining milk in a pan with the cream and sugar and heat gently while stirring, until almost boiling. Remove the pan from the heat; whisk the gelatine into the cream mixture and whisk until dissolved. Leave to cool for 5 minutes and then stir in the amaretto.

3 Pour the mixture into the moulds and chill until set (about 4 hours). Unmould and serve with Ruby Sauce.

4 To make Ruby Sauce: Place the sugar and 1 cup (250 ml/ 8½ fl oz) water in a pan and stir over medium heat until the sugar has completely dissolved (do not allow to boil). Add the cinnamon stick and simmer for 5 minutes. Add the raspberries and wine and boil rapidly for 5 minutes. Remove the cinnamon stick and push the sauce through a sieve; discard the seeds. Cool and then chill the sauce in the refrigerator before serving.

NOTE: If you prefer, replace the amaretto with ½ teaspoon almond extract. The Panna Cotta will be a little firmer. This is delicious, and traditionally Italian, with fresh figs.

TIRAMISU

Preparation time:
30 minutes + chilling

Total cooking time:
Nil

Serves 6–8

INGREDIENTS

- 3 cups (750 ml/26 fl oz) strong black coffee, cooled
- 3 tablespoons dark rum
- 2 eggs, separated
- 3 tablespoons caster (berry) sugar
- 250 g (8¾ oz) mascarpone
- 1 cup cream (250 ml/8½ fl oz), whipped
- 16 large savoiardi biscuits (cookies)
- 2 teaspoons dark cocoa powder

1 Put the coffee and rum in a bowl. Using electric beaters, beat the egg yolks and sugar in a small bowl for 3 minutes, or until thick and pale. Add the mascarpone and beat until just combined. Fold in the whipped cream with a metal spoon.

2 Beat the egg whites until soft peaks form. Fold quickly and lightly into the cream mixture with a metal spoon, trying not to lose the volume.

3 Dip half the biscuits (cookies), one at a time, into the coffee mixture; drain off any excess and arrange in the base of a deep serving dish. Spread half the cream mixture over the biscuits (cookies).

4 Dip the remaining biscuits (cookies) and repeat the layers. Smooth the surface and dust liberally with cocoa powder. Refrigerate for 2 hours, or until firm, to allow the flavours to develop. Delicious served with fresh fruit.

STORAGE TIME: Tiramisu may be made up to 8 hours in advance. Refrigerate until required.

RICOTTA POTS WITH RASPBERRIES

Preparation time:
20 minutes

Total cooking time:
25 minutes

Serves 4

INGREDIENTS

• 4 eggs, separated
• ½ cup (125 g/4⅓ oz) caster (berry) sugar
• 350 g (12¼ oz) fresh ricotta
• ¼ cup (35 g/1¼ oz) finely chopped pistachio nuts
• 1 teaspoon grated lemon rind
• 2 tablespoons lemon juice
• 1 tablespoon vanilla sugar (see NOTE)
• 200 g (7 oz) fresh raspberries

1 Preheat the oven to moderate 180°C (350°F/Gas 4). Beat the egg yolks and sugar in a small bowl until pale and creamy. Transfer to a large bowl and add the ricotta, pistachio nuts, lemon rind and juice and mix well.

2 In a separate bowl, whisk the egg whites into stiff peaks. Beat in the vanilla sugar, then fold into the ricotta mixture, stirring until just combined.

3 Lightly grease 4 individual, 1-cup (250 ml/8½ fl oz) ramekins. Divide the raspberries among the dishes and spoon the ricotta filling over the top. Place on an oven tray (sheet) and bake for 20–25 minutes, or until puffed and lightly browned. Serve immediately, dusted with a little icing (powdered) sugar.

NOTE: You can buy vanilla sugar at the supermarket or make your own. Split a whole vanilla bean in half lengthways and place in a jar of caster (berry) sugar (about 1 kg/ 2 lb 3 oz). Leave for at least 4 days before using.

MIXED NUT BISCOTTI

Preparation time:
30 minutes

Total cooking time:
45 minutes

Makes about 50

INGREDIENTS

- 25 g (¾ oz) almonds
  (see VARIATION)
- 25 g (¾ oz) hazelnuts
- 75 g (2⅔ oz) unsalted pistachios
- 3 egg whites
- ½ cup (125 g/4⅓ oz) caster
  (berry) sugar
- ¾ cup (90 g/3¼ oz) plain
  (all-purpose) flour

1 Preheat the oven to 180°C
(350°F/Gas 4). Lightly grease
a 26 × 8 × 4.5 cm (10½ × 3 ×
1¾ inch) bar tin and line base and
sides with baking paper. Spread
the almonds, hazelnuts and
pistachios onto a flat baking tray
(sheet) and place in the oven for
2–3 minutes, until nuts are just
toasted. Leave to cool. Place the
egg whites in a small, clean, dry
bowl. Using electric beaters, beat
egg whites until stiff peaks form.

Add the sugar gradually, beating
constantly until the mixture is
thick and glossy and all the sugar
has dissolved.

2 Transfer the mixture to a large
mixing bowl. Add the sifted flour
and nuts. Using a metal spoon,
gently fold the ingredients
together until well combined.
Spread into the prepared tin and
smooth the surface with a spoon.
Bake for 25 minutes. Leave to
cool completely in tin.

3 Preheat the oven to 160°C
(315°F/Gas 2–3). Using a sharp,
serrated knife, cut the baked loaf
into 5 mm (¼ inch) slices. Spread
the slices onto the prepared
trays (sheets) and bake for about
15 minutes, turning once halfway
through cooking, until the slices
are lightly golden and crisp.
Serve with coffee, or a sweet
dessert wine.

STORAGE: The biscotti will
keep for up to a week in an
airtight container.

VARIATION: Use any combination
of nuts, or a single variety, to the
weight of 125 g (4⅓ oz).

WEIGHTS AND MEASURES

Weights and measures differ from country to country, but with these handy conversion charts cooking has never been easier!

Cup Measurements
One cup is equal to the following weights.

Ingredient	Metric	Imperial
Apples (dried and chopped)	125 g	4 ½ oz
Apricots (dried and chopped)	190 g	6 ¾ oz
Breadcrumbs (packet)	125 g	4 ½ oz
Breadcrumbs (soft)	55 g	2 oz
Butter	225 g	8 oz
Cheese (shredded/grated)	115 g	4 oz
Choc bits	155 g	5 oz
Coconut (desiccated)	90 g	3 oz
Flour (plain/self-raising)	115 g	4 oz
Fruit (dried)	170 g	6 oz
Golden syrup	315 g	11 oz
Honey	315 g	11 oz
Margarine	225 g	8 oz
Nuts (chopped)	115 g	4 oz
Rice (cooked)	155 g	5 ½ oz
Rice (uncooked)	225 g	8 oz
Sugar (brown)	155 g	5 ½ oz
Sugar (caster, berry)	225 g	8 oz
Sugar (granulated)	225 g	8 oz
Sugar (sifted, icing)	155 g	5 ½ oz
Treacle	315 g	11 oz

Oven Temperatures

Celsius	Fahrenheit	Gas mark	Celsius	Fahrenheit	Gas mark
120	250	1	200	400	6
150	300	2	220	430	7
160	320	3	230	450	8
180	350	4	250	480	9
190	375	5			

Weight Measures

Metric	Imperial	Metric	Imperial
10 g	¼ oz	300 g	10 ½ oz
15 g	½ oz	330 g	11 ½ oz
20 g	⅓ oz	370 g	13 oz
30 g	1 oz	400 g	14 oz
60 g	2 oz	425 g	15 oz
115 g	4 oz (¼ lb)	455 g	16 oz (1 lb)
125 g	4 ½ oz	500 g	17 ½ oz (1 lb 1 ½ oz)
145 g	5 oz	600 g	21 oz (1 lb 5 oz)
170 g	6 oz	650 g	23 oz (1 lb 7 oz)
185 g	6 ½ oz	750 g	26 ½ oz (1 lb 10 ½ oz)
200 g	7 oz	1000 g (1 kg)	35 oz (2 lb 3 oz)
225 g	8 oz (½ lb)		

Liquid Measures

Cup	Metric	Imperial
¼ cup	63 ml	2 ¼ fl oz
½ cup	125 ml	4 ½ fl oz
¾ cup	188 ml	6 ⅔ fl oz
1 cup	250 ml	8 ¾ fl oz
1 ¾ cup	438 ml	15 ½ fl oz
2 cups	500 ml	17 ½ fl oz
4 cups	1 litre	35 fl oz

Spoon	Metric	Imperial
¼ teaspoon	1.25 ml	$\frac{1}{25}$ fl oz
½ teaspoon	2.5 ml	$\frac{1}{12}$ fl oz
1 teaspoon	5 ml	$\frac{1}{6}$ fl oz
1 tablespoon	15 ml	½ fl oz

Index